Blooming Beyond Brooklyn

Poems of Roots, Sorrows, & Lessons

To Larry,
May your life continue to bloom in many delightful ways.
I'm delighted to have had a chance to "meet."

Iris J. Arenson-Fuller

Fondly,
Iris

Printed in the United States of America

First Printing, 2019

ISBN 978-0-692-03614-3

Cover design by Yvonne C. Espinoza

"Reading through the poems offered in this gorgeous collection, I immediately felt all the passion and heartache, joy and pain that fueled and fed every last syllable. Arenson-Fuller's words tell us a story to be sure, but the story appears in small doses of bright, beautiful light, like diamonds rediscovered within a long-forgotten cave. Though thoroughly impressive each on their own, together they shine with seasoned expertise from a true veteran of her craft."

-Sean Patrick Brennan, author of forthcoming novel, *tree house down,* *The Angel's Guide to Taking Human Form,* **and others.**

***

"Iris J Arenson-Fuller's poems are alive with authenticity and rich sensual language. To use the last line of one of her own poems, in this work there is the magic "of words gifted to us from gods that visit in only the dreams of a very few."

–Joan Kantor-award winning poet, author of *Fading Into Focus,* **a memoir about Alzheimer's and a changing mother-daughter relationship, as well as numerous other published works.**

***

"What I appreciate most about Iris's poems is their willingness to view rarely considered detail; see it freshly and with uncommon purpose. Or perhaps it is that her poems are unafraid to employ what is often considered mundane or common and in doing, they have mastered some kind of alchemy by transforming the everyday into thoughtful and multi-layered works of connection and credence. This is rarely done as skillfully, or with as much heart. Her poems are current and at the same time reach beyond what is current. They startle and soothe simultaneously."

–Bob Vance, award-winning poet, essayist, playwright, social worker, life coach, photographer
***

"Here is straight talking poetry yearning for the idealism and optimism of youth, not for selfish reasons, but for the opportunity and time to defeat hatred and intolerance. Time passing drives the writer unwillingly to 'leave the battlefield' (What Is Already Exploding) but also brings impatience with those who do not respond quickly enough and 'do not hear the drumming in the night'. Frustrated but still driven to engage in progressive struggle Arenson-Fuller appeals strikingly 'Let me show you the wisdom caught up in my hair'. (Before The Light Drops).
Intolerance and tragedy too often occur within a close family, another arena that Arenson- Fuller does not shirk from entering. Richard 'thinks about his father shouting' then 'picks up the needle and stops thinking forever at 24 years.' (At 24 Years).
This is tough stuff straight out of Brooklyn from a poet who pulls no punches. I like it."

-David Subacchi, poet based in North Wales, (UK) author of five collections in English and one in Welsh. *Where Is Wales?* His newest, was published in January 2019

DEDICATION

I have finally had the time and courage to put together a poetry collection that is part memoir and part imagination. It has taken me a long time and I've gotten sidetracked along the way. The span of years behind me is now so much greater than the one ahead. I figured it was time! It may be good that I waited so long to do this. My longitudinal view allows me to see the blessings in my life so much more clearly now. The sorrows still intrude, but I have made space for the lessons learned and for the joy to dance freely through my days.

I dedicate this book of poems first to all of my family.

> ~To my husband Art, to my adult kids, Jesse, Crispin, Ben and Helena, who have often had to put up with someone whose head was in the clouds fishing around for new ideas to pull down and write about, or who was wrapped around problems I didn't need to solve but thought I did. I thank my daughter-in-law Yvonne, for her patience and help.

> ~ To my two lovely granddaughters, grown-up Tasya, and young Gabriella, who represent hope and wonderful possibilities.

I also dedicate this book to all of my loved ones and friends who are now gone. Sadly, there are too many to name. By being part of my life, they have enabled me to find richness in an imperfect world and to understand that it's my responsibility to do whatever I can to make that world just a little kinder.

~To my clients, past and present, from my decades of running an adoption agency, and now as a Life and Loss Transformation Coach…You have given me the incredible gift of sharing your deeply personal hopes, dreams and goals, and entrusting me to help you find or create what you needed.

Thank you!

Iris J. Arenson-Fuller
Bloomfield, CT

CONTENTS

A Message from the Author for Non-Poetry Lovers

I have a request. If you bought this book because you know me and wanted to be supportive, I truly appreciate that. If you think you don't like poetry or understand it, please read it with an open mind. Be prepared to challenge your past assumptions about yourself. I think (hope) you will actually discover that you *do* like poetry. You are likely to find that things take on new meanings when they are read a second or a third time.

I strive to create poetry that can be enjoyed and felt on different levels. I try to write poems that touch the reader and evoke feelings and experiences he or she has had. To those who want to find meaning on a more profound level, go for it! I don't enjoy sitting and discussing my poetic intentions or dissecting my work with anybody. I tired of doing that when I was young and am long past my student days now. I leave such discussions to eager, young MFA candidates and grads (No offense, I hope, to those MFA grads who may well be editors to whom I have submitted or intend to submit work).

The Author's Story

This collection is really a memoir in many respects. There is a lot of pain and angst that went into some of these poems, but they also document the hope and growth that blossomed in me over time. I have lived on both the dark and bright sides of the universe. Most of us have by the time we reach mature adulthood, and certainly by the time we become senior citizens. I have experienced great joy too, in spite of having had bleak and challenging times.

I have been writing almost my entire life, since shortly after the age of three when I first learned to read. My work has appeared in some literary magazines and a couple of anthologies, but for many reasons, I have not put together a collection before. I have written pretty steadily, with only a few lapses here and there at especially busy or traumatic periods of life. The esteemed writer, Langston Hughes, presented me with a poetry award when I was in high school. He asked me to pledge that I would never stop writing. I made the same promise to my father. I mention this, not for the purpose of name dropping, but because it remains one of the happy highlights of my life.

Writing has been a way to reanimate on some level, the cherished people who were and are in my heart. Writing has enabled me to express things I could not always do in other ways. When my kids were growing up, they used to complain that I was the only mother they knew who wrote them letters, though we lived in the same house.

Of course, I did not begin writing as a small child because I knew it would be a vehicle for me to process difficult feelings and thoughts. The ability to put things on paper guided me through tough times, perhaps as much as therapy and coaching, two different but compatible approaches to helping people learn to be stronger and better versions of themselves. I have had to reinvent my life a few times now. The constants at those times were my writing, family, the need to have a strong purpose, and to put something back into the world. I have learned how to honor the past without becoming consumed by it. I have helped my clients do this in my work as a Life and Loss Transformation/Life Reinvention Coach.

I have had a coaching practice, Vision Powered Coaching, since early 2009. When clients are willing, I sometimes use writing exercises to help them articulate and clarify many things as we work on their goals during important passages or life transitions. I have discovered that coaching work and writing have some things in common. They both help people discover what is already within them that is yearning to be liberated, bringing it out into the open to serve them as they make the changes they desire.

I write about a lot of topics, but this collection, in particular, is about loss, growth, life passages, and things I have learned. There is quite a bit of sadness in the poems, yet I hope readers will find something beneficial and relatable in the observations and emotions. I hope some of my life lessons and the joy in those lessons will also come through.

I have worked hard to learn how to get past constant bemoaning about my misfortunes and to appreciate my blessings. I am not suggesting this comes naturally to me. I admit I am still a work in progress. I have discovered the benefits of gratitude. This is a buzz word nowadays, but has been very important in my ability to move forward and to find meaning and purpose. I am not really a religious person, but one of my favorite prayers is one from my Jewish heritage, the *Shehechiyanu Blessing*, which thanks the Creator for having blessed and sustained us and for enabling us to reach this season.

My first husband, Kim, died in a tragic fire when he was 38 and I was 35. My kids and I also lost most of our material belongings. We had no permanent home for about a year. When we moved back into our restored home, I posted the *Shehechiyanu Prayer* on the wall next to my bed, so it was the first thing I saw upon awakening. It gave me courage and peace. It helped me to remember the blessings I still had. It helped me to understand that everything that has happened to us, and to our loved ones no longer with us, is very much a part of who we are in the present moment. This gives us strength and insight we might never have acquired otherwise.

I had also lost my brother, father, nephew and a very close friend not long before the fire in which Kim died. For several years before that, my kids and I had shared the colossal anguish that Kim went through as he dealt with the betrayal of his body, piece by piece, due to rapidly progressing multiple sclerosis. I was filled up with my own fury at the time, at the loss of our future and the dreams we had dared to dream when young and highly idealistic.

Over time, I saw that we must actually choose to feel better and to live with gratitude. Once we realize that, our perspective shifts. Then we figure out how we will carry out that choice, step by step. We can use our unique personal knowledge, experience, and talents to make our lives and the world a little better. We each do that in our own way, but I believe that is the only way to move beyond mere survival and to truly live your life

I think I always knew instinctively that my sadness, once expressed, and worn until it became a familiar part of me, would slowly wear thin and some light would eventually shine through its fabric. However, I knew I could not just ignore the hurt and pain.

Years after being widowed, I adopted a fourth child. When she was two, I met and five years later, married my dear husband, Art. A period of other hardships followed, with illnesses, caregiving and losses of my mother, sister, more friends, dear clients and cousins. Later, we lost Art's brother, mother and other beloved relatives. Life has taken us in many directions and taught us many things. I have been so fortunate, despite the hardships.

I understand now how the qualities of my ancestors and their passions and views have been incorporated into my life. This is evident in my political beliefs, my respect for my cultural roots (which I did not have when younger), and my interest in human rights. I am sure that my lifetime infatuation with language and with poetry in particular, came from my father and my uncles, who did not have much formal education, but who respected and admired the literary arts.

Our loved ones definitely do live on in us in so many ways. I am proud of the work accomplished by the non-profit adoption agency I co-founded with my first husband, and which I ran for about thirty years. He lived only six months after our initial licensure. He did not live to see our first child placement, yet I know the work that was carried on for so long was a beautiful and living tribute to his memory. We established a fund within the agency called the Gertrude and Harry Arenson Family Builder's Fund, set up in honor of my parents, to assist people with some extra expenses entailed in adopting special needs kids.

When, on an inspiring autumn day, I am enchanted by the colors in the landscape, I consciously find myself thinking of my father and almost seeing through his eyes. I remember his love of photography and how he found magnificence in everything. He knew beauty and pathos walked side by side in every aspect of life. Both happiness and sadness moved him to tears, but laughter also came easily to him. He found something humorous in nearly every situation. He felt things deeply. He loved music and particularly opera and classical music. As I have aged, I have deliberately thought about him and have tried to emulate his appreciation for life.

From my mother, I have gained a sense of loyalty, of the practical, and an ability to search for simple, utilitarian tools of survival. What I rejected in her as a child and teenager has become a part of how I do things now, with *"practical heart,"* like both my mother and my father. That practicality and work ethic has served me well.

As a child, teen, and young woman, I felt loved, protected, and even admired by my family of origin. I didn't always feel heard or understood. I know a lot of young people feel that way. I was rebellious and sometimes unappreciative of my family, though they managed to support me through various choices and ventures that were frequently confusing or alien to them. I could not wait to leave what I thought of as the prison of Brooklyn, New York, and to begin to explore new areas of the U.S. and other countries. Sadly, it took me many years and many losses to finally appreciate the family with which I had been gifted, and the love and values they instilled in me.

In modern Western society, many people foolishly think we have to "forget and move on". If you have lost a loved one, you know that we don't really forget or recover, and our grief marches beside us.

There is one other thing I want to add. As I was finishing this up, my youngest daughter, Helena called. She asked what I was doing. I told her I was writing a section for my poetry book. Her response was, "Why can't you ever be doing elderly-type things? You're always working on something. Why can't you be a Senior Knitizen?" Of course, she was joking (I think), but I hope that she and my other adult kids, as well as my grandkids, will one day find things about me that they want to honor and incorporate into their lives after I am gone!

"Your absence has gone through me

Like thread through a needle.

Everything I do is stitched with its color."

— **W.S. Merwin**

Iris J. Arenson-Fuller

Brooklyn Summers

On adolescent summer strolls through native habitats
I often felt like an alien waiting to be freed
of pain I thought rested only in poet bones,
like mineral deposits in hard city water.

Walking through multi-lingual chattering streets
littered with paper cups from candy store frappes
I desperately wanted to escape to a new world
beyond Brooklyn, where I felt loved but unheard.

On those scorching sidewalk fried-egg days,
Brooklyn felt as barren to me as this old womb.
Avenues were alive, teeming with every shade
of scurrying human paint chips, all strangers to me

all avoiding eye contact whenever possible.
The knishes and cannoli I loved are still there
to taunt weight watchers and I can even taste them.
Those I eat today are sadly Connecticut bland.

Brooklyn stoops are now empty of long-dead neighbors
who sat on benches in front of their tiny row gardens,
delighting in casual summer gossip, tattling to parents
on naughty teen girls caught holding boys' hands

or putting on makeup after leaving their houses.
Photos of Mrs. Epstein, Mr. Pachuto, Mrs. Scaletti,
live in greying album pages, buried under boxes
in the basements of descendants.

My old stoop on 70th Street must be crumbling now,
or perhaps craves the comforting bounce of a pink ball,
Spaldine, of course, a pleasure it can still remember,
along with the stomp of my tired father's work shoes
and eager young lovers giggling and kissing.
I barely remember them, though I was one,
moving methodically through willing boys
like boxes of Cracker Jacks.

My Brooklyn summers are only sweet flashbacks
and faded photos of folks no one knows but me.
If I immerse them in water, they may swell
and come to life like sea monkeys.
Nothing really changes but perspective.

Contradictions

This Sunday morning is cinnamon and sorrow
sending me those dot-dash memory messages
of things that were, things that still need doing,
things left unsaid, words waiting for natural birth.
I wrestle with life's contradictions, sometimes winning,
sometimes on the ropes or knocked out cold.

Life is like my mother's scented pillows,
the ones she made those summers in Kerhonkson
when she complained about socks to be darned,
but sat in the swing chair under the trees
stuffing small pillows with fresh pine needles.
I bet if your head has ever rested on a pine-filled pillow,
has ever sought sanctuary from day's decisions,
then you will know exactly what I mean.

There's no way to describe the coupling of sharpness
and clouds, of woodsy clearness mixed with
a slightly unpleasant smell of earthen mystery.
There's no way to explain how something that comforts
can sting and also cradle your weary head with sweetness.
That, simply put, is the story of my life,
and maybe yours too.

When To Let Go

When the heart feels squeezed and wrung dry
when grief layers are like phyllo dough
oozing with bitter fillings of inky misery
when they tell us poems of loss are clichéd
I sit by the pond of old sorrows trying
not to hear oily, useless words floating
over the surface of pain.

When I speak to the trees, I ask them how
they know when to let go, when to shed
leaves once promise-green and tender
that burst without warning into sudden flames
of screaming color and finally succumb
as winter charges in and takes them all away.

How do trees and humans know what to do
when seasons of life rush past, waving,
when children zoom by on carousel horses
laughing with joy as we stand by the gates
wishing we could climb up on those
painted steeds to grab a brass ring?
Some things we just know.

So when the sun's face sinks behind
the pines on the nearby wooded path
it's time to rise, to stretch stiff limbs
to gather up book and half-eaten apple
to give one more long, hungry look
at our pond, at persistent wildflowers
lingering at water's edge, at geese
thinking of their coming journeys,
while our eyes drink the honey
as long as we can, grief or no grief.

4

Gertie Sews

My mother sews without a needle
fingers making birdbeak stitches
in the hem of the dress
on her tiny body.
My mother wants me to buy cookies and coffee.
She imagines her old kitchen table
with plates of goodies,
instead of the electric bed and call button.

My mother calls me her sister.
Doesn't remember that her sister
died last year.
My mother stitches scraps of life
asleep and awake.
The needle moves in and out of her mind.
She binds us all till we are stuck
like nuts on honey cake.

We lift our fly legs and wave them,
though we never escape.
Long after she leaves us, she waits quietly
under her kosher made-in Israel shroud
hoping that Carol and I are together
still waving our tiny legs, holding each other's
wrinkled hands, mine looking just like Mama's
with her two rings staring.

We are not together.
Only I am here now, the baby
who hates to sew and always has.
I am learning to make the needle airborne.

The needle zooms, stitching together memories.
I see our bunk beds, the breakfast nook,
my father's sweet Williams in his tiny garden,
my sister in her first evening gown,
my *Zaide* admonishing his grown sons,
my *Bubbe* fishing for compliments,
the other *Bubbe* chopping nuts and apples
in a wooden bowl, with sounds of singsong
praying in the background,
in the kitchen with the four-legged sink
in Boro Park.

I sew together all of the births, the baby smells,
the hard-boiled eggs and whitefish salads
after the funerals.
My hands are stiff and tired but I sew together
the sound of my brother's voice shouting at my father
with love sadly hiding under the noise,
the gifts my father always gave my mother,
wrapped in silver paper, stacked to the sky.

The piles of necklaces and earrings overflow
into streets I see, but cannot find or follow.
I sew my brother's prosthetic leg to my first husband's
wheelchair cushion,
a portrait of my father's lit-up face listening
to my poetry.
I sew my mother's eyes to mine.
I sew until I run out of invisible thread.

I sew until all of this is stitched up tightly
in a giant ball I will never be able to unravel,
that rolls behind me wherever I travel,

a ball of light and dark, a huge black and white
cookie from the corner bakery, just for me.
I don't yet know whether to eat it, or keep it in a box,
to wear it, or feed it to my granddaughter.
So I just sew.

At 24 Years

I was busy making decisions about
creating future generations, about my
responsibility to curtail overpopulation,
to unite strangers and their gene pools,
to make a song, "Black and White Together,"
the new anthem for our family.

Our Richard is just blocks away from home
with a so-called friend in a Brooklyn walk-up,
seated on a torn, plastic slipcovered blue couch,
memories of rehab in CT, still fresh like Sunday
bagels from Izzy's on 18th Avenue, promises made
only hours ago, heavy on his chest along with the
lingering weight of corned beef and mustard on rye.

He thinks about his father's shouting,
the decorative copper plates rattling
on the living room wall, his mother's tears,
her hands over her ears as he unveiled
the truth about his secret sexual choices,
thinks of his taciturn teen brother upstairs,
shutting out his confessions with loud music.

He imagines himself that coming Monday,
in a lonely cubicle, his first day on the job,
his fresh start as a government office flunky,
behind a brown metal desk, several coffee stains
on the old blotter no one has bothered to discard,
and he picks up the needle and stops thinking
forever, at 24 years.

Mandel Broidt (Mandel Bread)

Gertie was no master European pastry chef
creating glorious golden strudels or pies of scraps
and wishes from the cupboard and ice box.

That was her mother, rotund, sweet-faced,
a flower in her hair, large drooping breasts
hiding under the full-length patterned apron.

Gertie's mother gathered ingredients in the apron,
holding it out gently like an ancient treasure,
carrying baking bounty from pantry to work table.

Grandfather prayed and swayed in the next room
droning, bending, sniffing as wife sifted,
rolled, pinched, conjured up sweet miracles.

Did she think of Romanian campfires, of gypsy
remedies while magic and surprises hovered
in her kitchen, invisible vibrating hummingbirds?

My mother planned and measured, pounded dough
into resignation, beat the white floury, eggy mess
till what made no sense sighed,
assuming the order she needed to feel safe.

Mama's kitchen was unlike mine,
with things spilling, minds of their own,
jumping from blue glass bowls, creating chaos.
Her kitchen was sparkling, predictable, as she knew the
real world never was, never would be.

On clear, cold nights, when we all went outside
to watch for shooting stars, she studied recipes,
chopping precisely, never adding odd tidbits
stashed in cupboards of imagination as I would.

She hummed the song, *Ramona* from the days
she and my father courted, hummed so softly
that the dog sleeping by the table could barely hear.

When perfect crisp logs emerged, never lopsided,
there was more measuring, then cutting and frosting.
Vanilla, chocolate, strawberry, in equal numbers.

Warm prizes peered out from the china plate.
Hands reached to unearth fruity secrets
while eyes found my mother's smile.

How well I remember the predictability
of us at table, counting chews, entering
Gertie's orderly world, where for that moment
we wanted nothing more.

Harry's Pictures -I

An image stuck on a beaded screen,
impressionistic smorgasbord of trees,
blood orange leaves
swaying in the wind.

Grapes on a vine, dark purple splats,
freshly painted white picket fence,
plumes of celosia, hot amber color
seen through a louvered window.

His favorite subject, country roads,
are abandoned, waiting to be photographed,
but Harry is gone, his slides suspended
in the projector.

He told me once, that when we die,
people we love move on along the calendar
and the dead watch running slide shows
of their lives, never realizing they are dead.

Words from his precious books marched
solemnly over an old covered bridge
in a photo, while we somehow continued
the tasks of living wrapped in a newly
muted blur of his colors.

Iris J. Arenson-Fuller

Harry's Pictures In Metal Boxes In The Downstairs Closet -II

It happens-that guilt settles on my chest
like the croup, but there's no sitting
in the shower in the night, inhaling
the steam for relief the way we used to
with the kids.

I really do want to dig out the long
metal boxes of slides, to free them
from burial under piles of cheap
Capodimonte candy dishes and ash trays
of various Brooklyn relatives, from bins
of trinkets that found their way to me
because I am it now, reluctant matriarch,
the Baby.

I think about it, but never free them from
the lonely prison of the downstairs closet,
can't bear the thought of finding those
brittle faded nothings resembling my
dimming memories that may one day
vanish forever.

What will I remember if I become
that wrinkled crone spooning soup
into her mouth, her nose, any orifice
that waits patiently to receive it?

Survivor's Tattoo

My survivor's tattoo is etched only in my brain.
You have not seen me in line at the gas chamber.
I was once a braided girl they thought too dark
to read without Braille dots, but they were blinded
by work day worries, bills to pay, and family feuds.

They loved with a tight grip, wanted me to stay,
so weeds grew wildly over understanding.
To them I was a bird in hand oddly aching to fly
far over fear-strewn petals on the unknown path
away from Brooklyn.

When I broke free, I flew like swirls of color
from an acid trip to the shimmering future.
Funnel clouds and winds lifted me to new worlds.

Now I try to create rituals, non-stop mind movies,
reels of long, silky threads that never stop,
of things they said and did, were and were not.
I recite their names, chants to those I loved
who climb in and out of poems after their deaths.
No longer the braided girl, but the tombstone scribe,
I catch words blowing down from the sky
like dandelion parachutes.

I am sometimes stuck in the ice block of memory,
chipping away from inside, wondering if the sun
which aids my task, will ever warm me.
What happens when I thaw, when my battery dies?
Will my Triple A membership be paid till I expire,
till someone else is hired as tombstone wordsmith?

Urges and Dreams

Awakening with the urges again,
stomach contracts, labor has begun.
You never ask for it to flow from
that murky, unseen dimension.
It runs from heart and gut,
like melted chicken fat.

It is your curse and blessing,
You must catch it as fast as it pours
now that is has returned to you,
amniotic fluid, enlarging into puddles
shaped like fat stars or cows.

You grab frantically for buckets,
reach for leaves, plates, whatever
your sleepy bones stumble over,
not wanting to waste one dewdrop,
because the words you betrayed
have found their way back to your dreams.

Will you be forgiven for abandoning them,
those words you knew first before your real life?
Before mother and father, dog or cat,
in pre-world when you could sit quietly
to find happiness, when words were no curse,
but bubbling gifts from a life within.

Storms and Wildfires

I watch the sad victims on the news,
tears and rivers flowing through streets.
I see bits of blue willow china floating
in runnels of tears, and amidst the debris,
a dog's dish, empty, beseeching the sky
for something to fill it, charred photos
melted heaps of memories, sobbing moms
clutching infants. I remember then!
My nightmares return, my body begins
its familiar, brief betrayal, reacting
in all the old terrifying ways.

These days, I *mostly* choose to refuse.
I don't want to live in a foxhole
forever on guard duty watching for
new heartaches that threaten to crash in.
I will not let joy be my hostage anymore.
I have learned to find the sweet spaces
in-between, where we sink in and marvel
at the peace, where we can sit watching
the trumpet lilies, peaches, pinks, delicious
marmalade spreading out over the day,
and we can choose to not be afraid.

When life looks like Maria or Harvey,
I admit I sometimes still wait for flames
to eat my life again or waters to rise,
but I argue with nightmares and let
good dreams float in like leaves
gently stirred by soft breezes, or like
a lover's touch, barely there,
promising greater pleasures.

What I Didn't Know When I Met Langston Hughes

Before I truly knew all living things were kin,
or that there was a larger menu of sexual preferences
than was served up in my family's small vinyl papered
kitchen with the orioles and jays staring at my soup.

Before I heard the first ugly name on my father's lips
after the neighbors scurried like tattling roaches
when they saw me riding in a rusted old car with six boys
and I cried hard from the stinging words,
a blue bruise painted in a bad dream by
Smokin' Joe Frazier's powerful fist.

Before I knew about toddlers in the ER at St. Vincent's,
whose limbs were mistaken for bacon strips
and burned in frying pans in kitchens where they should
have been eating freshly baked cookies.

Before I ever heard of Matthew Shepard, alone,
shivering in the cold, beaten, tied to a fence,
whispering, why into the brutal Wyoming wind.

Before I heard of napalm burns or Gulf War Syndrome,
of veterans who believed in their country, fighting
demons under city bridges, talking to themselves.

Before I grew up and out of a life that was bright,
textured like velvet, the nap never stroked in the wrong
direction but wrapped around me, warming me with
promises of poetry and young love.

Before my cave sanctuary turned into darkness where
I sat carving sad pictures of too many lost loved ones
or where I lay drenched in high-fevered sweats
unable to see a world that would be all right again.

Before that, I stood up, left foot asleep, limping across
a high school auditorium, pleated skirt, crisp white blouse,
high heels, ears with hoop earrings listening to loud claps,
tongues clucking with sincere pity for the pretty girl
they thought was crippled and about to receive
a poetry award from Mr. Langston Hughes.

Before that, I was pre-me and thought him merely
a rambling old man who foretold great joy and suffering,
extracting a shy promise that I would not stop writing,
even if life's pain took hold of my throat and choked me.
Four years later, he was dead and I still didn't know
what I didn't know when I met Langston Hughes.

***

(This poem was previously published in *Storybleed
Magazine*.)

Soup Solace

Through the kitchen window's colored glass,
few colors outside but an occasional dull sparrow
or flash of cinnamon chipmunk fur.

On these dark, wretched days, grief and dreams
fight for dominance and tie, while sanity swings
over the head, creaking and taunting.

Trained to mark beginnings with celebration dances,
sometimes the mind is stiffer than the body,
just won't go there even with prodding.

She seeks solace in the comfort of soup,
thick with relief, reassuring, homemade broth,
fussed over, fattened up with vegetables,
whatever lingers, begging to be added.

She imagines the spreading smells of well-being
so much craved, wafting out to chilly rooms,
small Scottie, asleep in a trance of doggie dreams
lifting scraggly head to stovetop, eyes hopeful.

Instinct shuts out paperwork piles, cajoling clients,
even wily words waiting to wrap around her brain
and turn themselves into poetry.

Swift action, deft knife motions, chopping,
becoming her new song of survival,
tapping out hypnotic melodies she must answer.

She thinks of a lobster falling asleep slowly
in a cradle of gently rolling water, lulled to its end,
as a friend prefers to cook them.

This pot of soup, coming to life, is an imagined home,
so holding nose, she considers jumping into the vat,
enjoying the spicy succor of pot liquor, happily sinking.
Soon soft sleep comes, and dreams of a future
nearly forgotten.

The Story Of When Brooklyn Met Taipei

I remember scallion pancakes, shyly eyed while
eating doughy, bland bread with humdrum jelly,
specially bought for me, ceremoniously presented
on cobalt plate, silver cross painted in the center,
due to a misconception of what all Americans liked.
This not-so-typical Brooklyn-born, too-young widow
seated at a huge round table with smiling nuns,
and kind, ivory-haired Fr. Francis, one hazy morning
in gentle, teeming Taipei. Before breakfast, I sat
respectfully through Chinese Mass, a red-headed Jew,
who had arrived bearing gifts for orphans and hosts.

Sr. R. wrote a letter to the poor widow's mother
long before travel, promising to guard, to protect,
not quite understanding how many worried lectures
had overflowed like Manischewitz, spreading fast
in grapey puddles on white linen cloth at Passover.
The well-intentioned nun never saw my Mama
wringing out her fears with a wet dishrag, praying
in Brooklynese-Yiddish, to keep baffling foreigners
from twisting my head or transforming my heart,
into strange, unrecognizable gruel, not fit for
her Jewish daughter, no matter how untraditional.

I recall the nun who guided me through street markets,
offering up tasty snacks, musk melons and dumplings,
and laughing as I declined chicken feet that had once
made me gag when floating in Bubbe's chicken soup
along with tiny unripened eggs from some poor
little star-crossed chicken's ovaries. We stepped aside
for animals to pass, stopped at stalls where hawkers

extolled straw hats, toys and one plastic red and black
musical lazy Susan, approved, wrapped in brown paper,
tucked under my arm by the insistent Sister, who declared,

"If you don't like it, give to your mother, or your daughter.
Good price."

Once home, I set the tacky musical lazy Susan on a bench,
where it lived, amusing children for maybe fifteen years,
slowly sounding more raspy, when one cold morning
after saying the Hebrew prayer for my then-dead mother,
I knew the plastic prize was finally ready for the trash.
The tale of how it came to me will be endlessly retold
until brain and mouth become strangers, till I am too
intent on eating pureed fruit to remember
either Brooklyn or Taipei.

Remembering Sr. Mary Holy Cart and Pondering Jewish Roots

I

Long ago, Mary Grace and I,
New England transplants from Brooklyn,
bought an ugly needlepoint picture for $1
at someone's yard sale.
We dubbed her Sr. Mary Holycart,
ungentle blue nun's eyes, under old-style habit.

Irish guilt won the wrestling match
so Jewish guilt, the loser in that game
got to take Sr. Mary home to live in a corner
forgotten by all but dust and cobwebs.
Who knows what happened to her?
Maybe tossed with old toys, chipped cups,
hippie jeans embroidered with yarn flowers,
crumbled friendships that grew stale as we aged,
adult consciousness that crept in unannounced,
deciding she might offend a visitor who spotted her.

II

I think Jews are a little like Marines,
or I am , anyway.
You know, "Semper Fi,"
no matter how we have roamed other spiritual paths
paved with interesting, unfamiliar stones,
exotic flowers poking out between the cracks.
We plucked wild blossoms
as we journeyed the decades,
far away from Brooklyn roots,
away from chicken soup with matzah balls.

No matter that we embraced more than men
who never wore skullcaps and prayer shawls,
who ate bacon, licked their fingers
with joyful waspish abandon,
renounced their own churches,
who loved the tales of Sholem Aleichem,
spewed Yiddish phrases like tender love songs
we remembered just long enough to teach them,
then packed them all up in pickle barrels
of briny distant memories.

We never imagined one day wanting
to unearth these, lovingly uncovering
each one, holding it to our hearts
like the memories of Passover dishes
unwrapped once a year, the glass ones,
along with the dog and cat black
and yellow salt and pepper shakers,
the white enamel pail for storing
hard boiled eggs, potatoes, Passover snacks,
the pan we used for making fried matzohs
while our neighbors put on Easter bonnets.

III

My brother-in-law, dying of brain cancer,
might smoke a turd in two hells
but I don't think there is a hell
in the books of my forefathers.
Baptized Catholic, later a Bar Mitzvah Boy,
(shhh, it's a big secret)
now as passive as his sweet, insecure mother,
who swayed like bamboo in winds of conflict,
who bowed to dictates of others, mostly men.

He wants to speak to a rabbi, but settles
for a priest his wife corrals in hospital hallway
and he even wears a crucifix for weeks.

We don't know what he is thinking, fearing,
have no knowledge yet of how it feels
when threads of death wind tightly around you,
pulling you closer and away from living.
We don't know what dreams swell up
next to the cancer and play back murky pictures
whether he wants to see them or not.
We don't know if the visions are soft promises,
pastoral paintings, or more like wild hijacking
of the senses after ingesting peyote mushrooms,
dreams of colors, or of shadows and ogres.

We do know he has asked three times for a rabbi,
perhaps a messenger from his grandmother's world,
papered with rules or singsong lessons learned as a boy.
He thought this world had been painted over,
but it slowly peels itself off the surface of his days
in crumbly strips, landing on couch, or wing chair
piled high with stacks of books and hats.
The grand piano we never heard played,
the cello, violin, the apartment crammed
with remnants of a life saved for someday
all watch, asking questions and answering
with more questions, like ancient Jewish scholars.

(This poem was previously published in the *Jewish Literary Journal*.)

What Is Already Exploding

Remembering days of nude calmness
in fields of green comfort under
Vermont sunshine when I was way
too young to fear skin cancer
or to know hatred would one day
invade my living room and grab
my country by the short-hairs.
I feared unjust wars then too
and hatred I thought I could help
wipe out like a blackboard eraser
because my generation was strong
because I was young and supple
filled up with love and dreams
as we lay watching clouds, or
shooting stars in a dark sky
talking all night about life, believing
we had answers to questions
we didn't even understand.
Now you are long dead, I am old,
wondering if there's time to do
half the things that race through
my head, that grab my heart.
I never give up, but today I notice
the piles of leaves decaying
in the yard and wonder how
to keep decay and destruction
away from those I love, and
from those whose minds somehow
navigate the rubble of rancor
yet close their eyes to what
is already exploding.

Machete Magic
Seeing Kim (October 1, 1943 -March 12, 1982)

I

I see him out in the yard, no shirt,
sun imprinting rays on naked back,
etching an Aztec calendar in skin.
The small silver one I bought him
used to tarnish from his acid sweat.
I made a ritual of polishing it.
From the kitchen window, I admire muscles,
bull neck, robust arms, thick, reassuring calves.
Machete in hand, he dances, attacks brambles,
strategizes against weeds that will not win.
A smile spreads, batter-like over his face,
oozing into hazel eyes, flecks of orange.
The mower in the shed sits, dejected,
expensive German steel he had insisted on,
push mower bought on one of many whims.
He refused to stand behind a power machine
along with the neighbor-clones.
He choreographs moves, muscles recalling
Zen football in Golden Gate Park, as he becomes
an artist, pretending to paint poppies with the blade,
but cuts them down instead, so for a moment,
he is sad, then resumes the planned offense.
Resting, he chugs water, between swigs, sings
a loud song hidden in his head from a years-ago
acid trip that made him laugh then, and still does.

II

One day he announces no more machete.
He wants vines and weeds growing fast,
crawling over doors, covering windows,
undulating snakes protecting us from outsiders,
blocking out wind and troubles that threaten chilled bones.
We are sweetly huddled together by the soapstone hearth
listening to endless Oz Tales on the worn striped couch
in the big white house on Unicorn Hill.
I think about machete magic, how it up and left.
When I tried to solve the trick of cups and balls,
no matter how fast my eyes raced to catch the magician
at his game, I saw the dull thud of death.
The magic just went away for too long, leaving a new
kind of joyless madness that paralyzed us all.
True, we survivors walked again, hanging on to trees
with thin bark, breath forming flimsy questions and sighs.
There were no miracle pills, but only time and light
sneaking in slyly through cracks in the armor.

III

When new fears swell, larger than Coney Island waves,
I cry and roar internal prayers that lips quickly change
(for survival's sake) to soft musical pleas.
I am mother, interloper by nature in their adult lands,
also founder and keeper of what was native and safe.
I can uselessly dig for maps that lead to fresh magic
till doomsday peeks through the bedroom curtain.
What hides in folds of invisible cloth is like Braille poems
waiting to be touched, but they must find their own cloth,
find the will to live without the aid of mother-midwife.

The machete rusts in the shed as I watch for Kim's ghost,
wondering if he sees us too, or wishes he could still
block out wind and troubles that threaten to chill bones.
My eyes seek light that is slow but will arrive.
I dream of us sweetly huddled together by the hearth
in the big white house on Unicorn Hill.

When We Are Afraid

Nightmares visit us
when we are afraid,
when we wear vulnerability
like designer pajamas,
when, in our waking state,
we are reluctant to look hard
at what we must do to leap away
from the tightness of now,
up into the wide open sky
of opportunity.

Tell yourself to breathe,
Breathe the spearmint air of woods
Breathe the spicy scent of Dianthus,
its mat of blue-green leaves,
a soft carpet for you to step on,
your path out
of your bad dream

Fear is a shadow puppet
from your childhood theater,
that's finally ready to crumble,
don't you think?
There is no demolition crew
collecting union wages.

You must place a green hard hat
on your beautiful head, to prepare
to awaken from years of ugly dreams
that have held you hostage.

Take apart the haunted, damaged building
but remember to salvage what is good,
what made you who you are.
Wake up sweet one, to my count of three.

Concentric Worlds

No, this is not a love poem,
not a way of wrapping us up
in a perfumed silk scarf with

gold embroidery that takes us
back to days when we inhaled
the scent of each other, thinking

of pleasure, of wildflowers, of pine
forests where we explored our
bodies on damp earth carpets

listened to wind tunes humming
softly in our ears, lullabies for
two young creatures just born

to a harsh new adult world,
oblivious to its looming dangers,
still seeing the woods as strong

guardian to all creatures nestled
under its sheltering green marquee
where birds practice their sonatas

I ask you then if this soft green
world is real and if the two lovers
reluctantly rising from damp ground

were ever really there, rolling in rhythm
to the small, scurrying beasts snapping
twigs as they rustled in the underbrush?

am I an actress in your vapory dream
on a journey in some distant past life?
are you a ghost lover who haunts

my house and heart nightly as I rudely
awaken in that cold sweat of longing
and reach for laughing empty spaces?

Mama, Jerry Says Jesus Got Alive Again

When Angela and I were child co-conspirators,
comparing barely budding breasts, we traded places.
Bribed with a dollar, I tumbled into her confessional
marking the start of my lifelong marathon seeking God.

This Jewish girl, quickly tutored, happily absolved,
bolted down those forbidden steps of St. Athanasius,
rushed out of Brooklyn with asthma and angst
into the hairy arms of one Mr. God after another.

When Anne Sexton's parachute of tortured poems
floated down onto my craggy teenaged landscape,
I devoured those poems devotedly, memorized
her messy map of angst and slashed arteries.

I marched with fat-assed pacifists from Queens
or stroked the flesh of young men resembling Jesus.
At night I prayed with spite to idols dancing wildly
in my adolescent imagination, while I sought truths.

Anne, your awful rowing to God took over my youth.
My throat was often sore from useless all-night debates.
You rowed while I ran, but we met in a thick suede fog
where poems dissolved in the foam of Sheepshead Bay.

Your rows of words kept you alive till they didn't.
Mine protected me, as I hurled myself to adulthood.
Years later, I was that same girl, though newly widowed,
that same Brooklyn braided kid with nightly nightmares.

I tried hard to obliterate dreams of scary carousel horses
shedding layers of paint, sheets of a husband's burned skin.
I remember now, how my small son clutched so tightly to
his dead father's picture, curls swinging, chirping softly,
        "Mama, Jerry says Jesus got alive again."

I remember handing him a cookie, which he ate,
not understanding it was my body and my blood.
I could not leave him, cookie crumbs and curls,
to climb my frayed rope of words and join you, Anne.

If God and I should ever meet in some unlikely place,
inside, a Brooklyn confessional, or in a man's embrace,
will I finally be resurrected? Will we debate all night,
two classic Jews with three different opinions?

I can see us now, two old cronies seated on a park bench,
drinking vodka till the morning light, my ultimate companion
at the end of the race. Not dead husband, or live husband,
not Apollo, or even you, Anne, who surely must have stopped
your awful rowing by now, dear.

Balm For Invisible Wounds

Guilt has feathers too
that open at the touch of a button,
sometimes buttons you forget you have,
that are often pre-wired.
We can see the feathers opening,
slowly spreading dark colors,
spilled ink soaking into souls.

These are not the iridescent feathers
of the peacock, screaming out glory
or nobility, but it depends too, on which
ethnic foods you eat and who sits
at the table when you wipe off
your greasy fingers and belch.

Buddhists can tell you peacock feathers
are steeped in meaning, and life offers us
its teas of renewal or its drinks of defeat
that we may choose from a tea chest.
We can be blinded by our own colors
when we spread our tails seeking admiration.

Now you must claim your ability to survive
even in the face of suffering.
I don't want our shared spray of guilt to mist
your heart, though I don't know how to help
you turn off the nozzle. Oh, this terrible guilt,
sometime wrapped tightly in genomes,
so much like cruel gnomes.

For you, I would sew more eyes
on the peacock's feathers,
make you watch the heavens cleave
to pour wisdom like a balm
for your deep, invisible wounds.

I would rip out your fears,
your feathers of vanity and guilt.

Next, I would perform a transplant,
I'd fill your skin with golden feathers,
then would watch you fan them out,
your heart once again uncluttered
as you let the light carry you back
to the brilliance, to the blues and greens
that once sat happily on your canvas.

Two Yolandas

My long-ago Yolanda,
Costa Rican mother, African father,
chestnut skin, cinnamon toast highlights,
amber eyes, gemstones with powers
never sensed or tapped, that cried
magical tears, of Phaeton's sisters.
She breezed into my classroom,
self-conscious, eyes downcast.
Soon friends, we practiced roles
for psychodrama class.

At her birthday party,
I was a nondescript white zircon
plunked down on a velvet tray of gems,
vivid, intense, overshadowing
this lone white girl.
There was Yolanda, shawl pulled taut
covering arms usually bare, but not
hiding bruises on cheeks,
amber eyes glowing through
two cobalt and red swollen splotches,
boyfriend perpetrator nowhere in sight.

She hugged me, sadly more mindful
of my comfort than of her own.
I wanted fierceness from her,
wanted her to erupt like an ugly typhoon,
angry at the one who did this,
angry at all in her path.

One year later, he killed her.
In my memory, her tears are still
washing onto the shore, true amber,
ancient fossil-mysteries trapped inside.

Yolanda II

On hilltops in the Philippines,
body bags are stacked in lumpy piles,
waiting for the humiliation of mass graves.
A Storm Queen merciless, ravished all
who dared to breathe, eat, or rock a baby
in the center of her wide path, as she
claimed her right to reign and ruin.

Now fast students of the science of mourning,
of living amidst rubble and cadavers,
of despairing, of remembering who and what was,
survivors wrap scarves around sad, stunned faces,
to ward off the putrid smells of death and begin
to measure existence in inches, in passed-along
tales of befores and afters.

I can't help thinking of my long ago Yolanda,
who was not a raging force of nature,
who did not claim her right to just be,
who stepped aside so harsh storms
and violent waves could beat her glow
into eternal submission.
I am bashful in my prayers.

Who am I to ask for things, even if not for myself?
Still, I pray for long ago Yolanda
whose name I always thought beautiful,
pray for those who must try to live again,
and for those whose tears are real,
burning their cheeks as they wait for help.

(*Two Yolandas* was previously published in *Into The
Void, Arts and Literature,* formerly in Dublin, Ireland
and now located in Canada.)

Lorca and His Crying Lizards

If lizards imbibed, I think they might yawn,
toss back one glass of dusky wine
after another, before sliding into sleep,
but they don't, so when they stretch out
on their bellies preparing for a siesta
and shed sloppy, shameless tears,
a small cactus nearby quietly sags
to the ground, its spiny carcass
unaccustomed to the deluge of moisture.

We were once like lizards soaking up sun,
innocently smiling at the he and she of us,
till we woke from our peaceful siesta
to nightmares lurking behind sand dunes,
breathing hot, fetid breath into our world.

Suddenly, I was a widow, growing deep roots
out of nowhere to tap sustenance for life.
I took off my wedding ring because I had to,
didn't lose it by accident, like Mr. and Mrs. Lizard.
I had no time to drown in a sea of my own tears,
or to sag to the ground unnoticed like the cactus.
What choice did I have but to rise from bed,
and throw off my leaden grief coverlet?

What choice but to leap with terror into
a new universe, oddly breaking no bones,
and letting life inject the glue to mend me,
even with permanent cracks still visible.
Let the lizards slumber in their parallel universe.
I filled out a change of address card, left the desert
and figured out how to find myself again.

In the Moment With Blue Glass

Don't misunderstand.
I love holding a cobalt blue glass
full of wine, love how the sun teases,
how the dust particles float, barely
visible, evasive, like the truths I used
to hold dear, that exploded, leaving
shrapnel on the heart.

Still, I must admire my blue glass collection
without getting stuck in the mud of memories,
murky, thick, threatening to suck me back
to a past that tries to hold me captive forever.
I want to fly ahead, to get lost in indigo beams
of color dancing madly, sparkling, as life
should be when we love and are loved.

I know what happens in moments of inattention,
when a wisp of a negative thought falls across
the face, a heavy, stale-smelling curtain.
How quickly sunbeams flee, afternoon shadows fall,
surrounding us with barbed wire, with armed sentries
that are only ourselves holding us back from living.
I have lived enough to know the padlock of the past
has a key sitting on a table on the planet of today.

If I peer into the future, make plans that fit my palm
as though I chose a perfect apple meant just for me
from a blue bowl of fruit on the oval kitchen table,
if I begin to count the ways I will win, not lose,
perhaps I will claim the gold in the rainbow's pot.

Or I might drop the blue vase waiting to greet a rose,
and spend my days picking up a million cobalt shards.

My hope, friends, is now in this moment of warm sun
projecting colors on a small spot of golden oak
where the lovely black Scottie dog is sleeping.

(Previously published in a different form in *Compass
Magazine, Kaleidoscope Section*)

Bee Guilt

I try to tell myself they're friends,
we need them,
I can't see myself as a terminator of life,
any life, no matter how small or delicate,
well, except that time before the invention
of the morning after pill long, long ago.
I even rush to rescue a shirtsleeve sticking
out of a drawer, feel the pain I may have
caused by my careless slam, even used to
rescue clothes hanging at back of closet,
fearing I had hurt their striped
or polka-dotted fabricy feelings.

I support all efforts to save our planet,
sign the right petitions my left wing ancestors
would be proud of, sense their loving eyes
smiling down on me through budding green
tree branches in my suburban yard that looks
nothing like their lower east side tenements.
I recycle, though every-so-often (don't tell)
do allow a brief guilty pleasure, sneaking a can
into waste bin, the plastic temptress under sink
but only when no one is looking, then sheepishly
I say an amended Jewish plea to any invisible
Redeemer and Savior who might be hovering
above my pretty New England kitchen.

I know all about recycling, about how life
recycles the pain and trauma forever
and each time we feel free, thinking
we have shed the heavy, moldy manteaux
that has kept us gasping for breath,
living in a rayless space of fear,
there it comes again to nip at our hearts,
so I carry that overpriced EpiPen, ready
to whip it out to stab my pasty white thigh,
but I see the bee circling, making threats,
and I attack it, waiting for the guilt to flood,
knowing it will and knowing fear has won again.

Honey Crisp Life

October tastes familiar and honey crisp
to the weary ones who wait for winter to invade.
We spot a leaf, prematurely brown and crackling,
and two suddenly bare tree limbs that lead us
up to holy destinations we no longer believe in.

Autumn air brings pleasure that's gone fast
like apple pie on a square white plate.
Golden breezes crunch in our teeth,
calling up our dreams of journeys
we have already paid for, but fear to take.

When we feel winter's breath on our necks,
it's far too hard to think of pre-need plans.
A small bird in the yard enjoys a tender worm
while life hides behind tall grass, sneering.
Soon our bird will shiver when winter reality stabs.

His tiny wings were strong just days ago,
soaring to places we can't imagine.
His feathered chest will hold in body heat
for a bit, and then his delicate wings
will become weak and gelatinous.

Sitting in a cup, our own needs are contradictions,
that taste like sweet and sour pomegranate juice.
If we don't empty the cup, the waitress pours it
down the drain, but if we do, the juice is still gone,
merely old scarlet memories trickling over bare skin.

We ask her what treats nature has written on the menu
and if there is possibly a senior special today.
She wipes away our questions with a sour dishrag.
Why do we tolerate her youthful impudence?
Why take her silence when life still seduces?

So no tip on the table for her, but for us,
at last, we find the crux of the matter.

Synesthete

A ruby red tablecloth, freshly ironed,
under the weight of alabaster plates,
sparkling wine goblets, puzzling fork array
as she settles napkin on lap, begging senses
to ignore, for once, the bitter taste of red,
the murky meanings of dark, crusty bread.
The others make small talk, chirpy chatter,
while she sips a cabernet, smiles deceptively
as bloody droplets fill her mouth with tastes
of sour recognition.

This is the bread of affliction her forefathers ate
when they were slaves unto Pharaoh in Egypt.
This is the Navajo fry bread ancient grandmothers
shaped with their weathered brown hands.
This is the Hoppin' John the women prepared
on New Year's Day for the family in the Big House
who waited with watering mouths, thin lips spitting
out molasses flavored thanks, chomping and slurping
juicy apple pie after the meal made with black hands.

This is the thick coppery fluid teasing wary lips,
blood hiding in gleaming crystal wine goblet,
playing an evil game with her ten thousand tiny
taste buds, longtime masters of ugly betrayal.
The other guests, will enjoy their crème brulee
as though it were just another caloric confection,
and not the glass shards of pain she tastes with
bitter images of women and toddlers exploding
near a suicide bomber in a back alley in Fallujah.

Iris J. Arenson-Fuller

Thoughts While Reading a Chinese Poem

Her word paintbrush stroked the image today
onto my mind canvas,
leaving stern, black characters to read
and to puzzle, as consciousness held
a conversation with itself.

For me to imagine her herons and seagulls
sleeping with heads tucked away is not hard.
They did not wish to see the men passing
by on the river. I have not always wished
to see the core of me.

I know how the wind can animate the body,
stir it, so skin flutters like leaves with no souls,
from repose to motion, how forces invade
causing disharmony of spirit, body and mind,
and I am finally ready for harmony.

I am excited about all of my big life lessons
coming into focus now that I am getting old.
My core wants to come out of its musty closet.
I embrace it, peeking through parted fingers,
daring to look long and lovingly.

I drift above the characters, watching the six
pernicious influences that create disharmony.
I am not afraid, but aware and flowing,
following the brushstrokes, my mind quiet,
knowing I have the power to be me no matter what.

Genetic Memory

No, you weren't always white, they sing,
their soft, thick, mysterious words falling,
into her curled shell ears, their sounds
echoing in her brain like crashing waves
till she knows she has heard them before,
stray liquid pearl words dribbling down
over open, parched lips, falling still further
onto sizzling desert sand near the big tent.
Her slight body shivers, soul silently begs
the tree-gods and goddesses to keep her safe,
to make new life from darkness and fear.

They cover her with colored cloths, orange,
red, to blend with blood, carrying her inside
the women's tent, they hold her very close,
breasts nearly smothering, singing sweet
caramel tunes, rolling her away, rolling back,
away again toward peaceful death, back again
to refuge in their strong, dark arms and melodies,
hugging her close, till she forgets who she is,
only remembering now who and how she
used to be, in another life, till she can hear
a ram's horn, as a new life pours forth.

Then she sleeps, someone whispers croons
to the new baby who is now her future.
She dreams of a basket floating on a river,
of standing on a platform in a market,
outstretched hands touching her, prodding
her like an avocado to check her ripeness.
Someone asks her name but she doesn't know.

49

She is in a truck with angry voices shouting
over a loudspeaker, the truck careening down
narrow lanes, women screaming, kids running,
infants falling from the mothers' thin arms,
disappearing quickly under huge truck tires.
She dreams she is a raven, flying in a starless sky.

No, you weren't always white, weren't always you,
yet always who you are, and distinctly different.
You are privileged, but you are also invisible,
free and shackled, sometimes dancing in the wind,
or straining at the ropes, fine red-blonde hair now,
marvelous black hair then, tall, an African crown,
and also dark, thick straight tresses hidden under
colorful scarf, wearing the hated Yuden armband.
Who are you really, woman?

EveryMother

This is for you
who rock your infant near the small willow tree
so the willow branches will menace any evil spirits.
You would place your child's spirit in a lotus heart
to protect her forever.
You will be her Goddess of Mercy for all her days.

This is for mothers lost, for mothers found,
for mothers who plant sparrow kisses on
their children's foreheads when they are burning
up with fever, or just napping on their laps.

This is for mothers whose wee ones are yanked
from trembling arms, sent to grow in foreign soil,
watered, tended, grown to adulthood by strangers,
for mothers who never know the children they bore,
but wish they had eleven ears to hear their cries
in distant places they may seek eternally, yet never find

This is for the portly mothers, and tiny mothers
who bake cookies with love, for those who marinated
in a sauce of hate as children, pouring this marinade
over tender offspring because they know nothing else.
This is for mothers who are accomplished chefs
and those whose sacred temples are fast food joints.

This is for mothers who try their best, but whose life
manuals are full of holes and indecipherable words
and mothers who soften the universe with goodness,
for mothers who helicopter, and those who weave wings.

This is for mothers whose wrinkled hands we hold
as we sit by their beds to feed them soup,
for the mothers we send flowers, for the mothers
on whose gravestones our love and poetry are carved.

This is for you, whose tykes run you ragged,
who leave you cheerio trails across the floor,
for you, whose sweet-smelling toddlers morphed
into adults living in some alien world you don't inhabit,
for mothers who are right now panting final solo breaths
before new life slides into the light.

This is for mothers who have lost children,
who find topical anesthetics to help themselves
grow into new days, but whose pain still cuts
like ground glass rubbed into the soul.

This is for mothers whose bowls have no fruit,
who weep to enter the land of motherhood,
but whose travels take them elsewhere,
and for all who are proxy moms,
yet love with full hearts.
This is for you,
EveryMother.

Seeking Elusive Brightness

when we feel the waves crashing against the windows
despite living in a land-locked town
sand grits up the mind, waves whisper secrets
not heard by others

it's time to bolt from rooms that engulf us in smoky dark
time to blink into the sun that warms sluggish earthworms
and tortured souls alike

time to do it when limbs are just long, pale pouches,
pounds of heavy pebbles sewn inside,
when our cell nuclei, not our ears hear the haunting music
of the evil snake charmer who tells us there
is no hope

if we don't force ourselves to exit, to find the light
our children will be orphans, forever dreaming
of unfulfilled promises that sit in a box upstairs,
memories fading much like lemon juice ink
on paper

we must seek elusive brightness under the veil,
must push out with the contractions
though the soul feels fragile, eerily unreal,
but I swear it's as real as your foot,
part of God's essence, impossible
to kill

who will keep repeating to us that all is temporary?
those who love us and think we won't listen?
the face in the mirror that knows the truth

but shrinks from it out of fear?
some guru, merely as human as we are,
though we resist our own humanity, fight the wind
with an inside-out umbrella, then just
 give up?

we sometimes learn too late that punishment
meted out by demons we create is far more ugly
than any real demons hiding under big rocks
those who believe in the Next World of Truth
will tell you even there, only the most wicked
make eternal payment

the average bear gets a ticket to watch life play back
to feel the pain of squandered potential keeping him
from Oneness but only till the lessons sink in and his
spirit is freed

it's time to bolt, urging unwilling limbs to move,
to unstick the needle caught in the groove
time to blink into the sun that still warms
earthworms, budding flowers and tortured
souls alike

if we force open those buds, risk living,
thumb noses at those who would try
to trap us into squandering our potential,
we will see spring flowers blooming
in dead of winter

Widower

They tell me that grief is forever
but guilt is like rotting fruit where
flies gather in circular pagan ritual
They tell me to weave a coat of poems
with threads that shimmer with hope
without any guilt in the pockets
so new life can grow from old sorrows

I can't seem to forget how I sat with you
felt every chemical blow to your too frail
body as though my long, clumsy limbs
were glued to yours, almost wrapped
in your skin, till you shook life loose
Now each new day is like a foreign film in
ancient Aramaic with no subtitles

My days are rayless, my nights
darker than the inferior human eye
can see, abyss without contour
Mornings find me by your window
where your perfect laughter made
flowers grow and birds joined your
song, unable to resist your music

Your loom is in the other room,
our room, a place my heavy feet
do not feel ready to find just yet
In my mind the door is nailed shut
though I've tried hard to pry it open
They say one day I will crash
through the barrier

Episodes In Which She Wakes In The Woods

She is old and well-seasoned now
like the ancient black cast-iron pan
she uses to render chicken fat with
its loud crackling that can distract
her attention momentarily from the
episodes that loop and confuse her.

Sometimes she does not sleep at all
sits alone in a silent, dark kitchen
listening to the ominous message
of a 50's teapot-shaped wall clock.

She can taste her young succulent stews
laced with wine, pungent with adventures,
expertly enhanced with rich, savory sex
when she sleeps and wakes in the lush forest.

She wears long dresses, digs up moist sorrows
and tender rhymes from under mossy patches,
as her friends all feast on their raw sorrows,
like dripping, youthful oysters.

Which part of life were those pebble-pathed,
fern-coated, wildflower-scattered days
in which she woke in the woods with
mythical creatures and bearded young men
who thought she was a moonchild, who gifted
her with blush pink moonstones to wear?

Wondering Where Life Went

No, I say!
I am giving you plenty of notice.

You won't find me in a chair,
stuck in a small room with that flowered paper.
You won't find me staring at the TV newscasters
I believe are my own family members
though I can't name any of them.

You won't be able to ignore me long enough,
so that one day you'll get a phone call
and learn I have just obligingly disappeared,
with only my crumpled old-lady's nightgown
left in a wrinkled heap on my recliner.

You won't catch me with that empty-eyed look,
picking and pulling at invisible gossamer threads
of memories that enter my head, but fall out onto my lap
because they have nowhere else to land, so instead,
I just pick unceasingly at my clothing.

You won't be listening to me singing a smarmy tune
some underpaid, relentlessly positive girl thinks
makes all old folks happy and docile, that a juke box
also once gifted me by mistake, a wasted 50 cents,
when I was searching for the screams of Janice Joplin.

You won't find me slowly disintegrating like rotted wood
on the window sill of your ancient house.
I am more dramatic than that.
I expect I will make a statement by breaking off
and landing with a big thud, so watch out.

You won't find me waiting patiently for a tray
of a cruel joke someone labels food,
tastes and textures scrambled together
No. No. My taste buds will always be shouting out
for delicacies, saffron rice and sublime soups.

In the scary hours of night, no wandering
strange corridors for me, desperately wondering
where life went, or who took it when I wasn't watching.
I plan to grab life, keep it with me on a wild ride
and to taste the wind on my face.

If I can't hypnotize words
into blind obedience and mold them into poems,
then I will be done and you will acquiesce
like those wayward words that try to escape.
I am giving you plenty of notice.

Before the Light Drops

How do I tell you all that I know before
the light drops and I can no longer fly,
before my wafery wings crumble into
a fine grime that you stash in a green jar,
glancing at it sometimes in the morning
when you eat oatmeal with Irish Crème.

I was moth before I was ever butterfly.
I was ordinary before I grasped that
I wasn't, but now am ordinary again
with nobody to admire the brilliant colors
I still prefer, even as decades parade by.

Who listens to old women?
Who runs excitedly to catch the words
falling from their mouths onto pages,
like tall grasses cut with sharpened scythe?
I need to tell you of the drumming in the night
that you young ones never seem to hear.
It rises up from lush forests I smell in dreams.

Let me tell you how to make the holy soups
of my grandmother's country where condiments
and melodious prayers embrace in mysterious union
to release longing we were unaware we had.
Let me show you the wisdom curled up in my hair
that I still brush daily, twisted arthritic fingers
demanding one hundred harsh strokes.

When Visitors Leave

She dreams of a flour blizzard
that flies up from the center
of the old yellow bowl
Her tongue is stuck fast to a spoon
She tries to jump through time
to travel to the deep blue before birth

Her seasons now drift together
as she sifts, the summer flowers
are waking up with their dewy faces,
their moist hopes soon turning to icicles

In one leap she is there, softly floating,
wondering where the voices are going
that grow more muffled and tinny
while they sit in front of her chair
speaking in tongues, strangers she thinks
she used to once know and love

She calls their names, smiles by reflex,
thinks of small children in blue mittens
throwing snowballs, laughing and then
the snow begins to heat and melt

They kiss her cheek, smooth her hair,
walk down the hall to the elevator
She cries out a name, not sure if
its's his. "Bob. Come back."
They go home to cry tired tears,
to feed the cat and wash the car
and she will dream again.

Fly Up

Fly up, old lady child, when the moon calls out.
You can't resist any more than your cousins
the inch worms can resist falling on braided heads
of screaming little girls underneath tree branches.
Your papery wings circle the majestic Tulip Poplar.
When you last traveled by, there were just three
blossoms nesting in her abundant long arms,
yet at dusk, after a hard day's work of eating
dainty holes in heirloom tablecloths and hats,
you see that Lady Poplar now has two thousand
blooms, as you sail above her green coiffure.
You don't stop to snack on her leafy buffet.
You were always a different sort of moth,
while she is known to be insect resistant.
You are rushing to see the yellow orb above,
to hear her haunting chants singing to you,
before her light and music fade at dawn.
Besides, you have less than a one-year life cycle.
Doesn't it seem like just yesterday that you were
so busy spinning silken tubes?
You must hurry past the songbirds you like,
past the scent of nectar that reminds your cells
of mysteries you know, though can't name,
before the moon stops crooning
and the blossoms tap-tap softly
onto the ground below, one by one.

We Are All Stardust

You crinkle your eyes, always a skeptic,
when I tell you there will be joy again.
I can read you well, always have.
Pain sits in the creases by your mouth.
Who found the recipe that has become you?
Who folded in the pain, the large cups of sorrow?
Who baked them in the sweltering sun
of your long, purposeless days?

When the sun punches out each evening,
you are lost and alone in a dark field.
That is what your eyes have adjusted to,
no longer discerning familiar, comforting shapes,
or paths that took you home to a place of safety,
to a place where she used to sit in her special chair.

You are trying to let in the starlight that teases
as it dances and flashes above your sad sky.
They tell you it's a must, though not how to do it.
This is a kind of brain damage no one understands.
Lessons about hope and peace struggle to push into
your heart, into your muscles so you can step forward.

Scientists say we are all made of stardust,
every part of us comes from a star.
We would not be here if a star had not exploded.
You would not be where you are, how you are,
if your life had not exploded, but look closely now
at what those star fragments have turned into,
watch where the Universe has sent them.
Will yourself to believe that amidst the rubble
of your explosion, there will be something precious.

The Guinea Pig Behind The Shed

We held a funeral service behind the shed,
respectful, next to the neighbor's interloping
rose bush and the pile of branches and brush
we never found time to haul away, that lived
there with our good intentions.

My lovely granddaughter Tasya's guinea pig,
Paprika, is remembered in this poem.
That is one of my jobs, I think, to find words
to keep loved ones with us at least a little,
when they try to float away to wherever it is
the dead go.

In that spot, years before, one lone sunflower
and one robust tomato plant strangely grunted
out of the ground.
We never witnessed conception or birth.
There was no midwife to coax them
into brave new worlds - Just as I had
no soul standing lovingly by to catch me,
no guru to show me the ways of widowhood.

One July morning, months beyond re-nesting
in our new, old house after the fire,
as we slowly wove in fresh twigs and bits
of straw among the memories, they appeared,
tomato and sunflower, behind the shed,
waiting to be discovered.

We had not planted that spot in years,
Still, there they were one morning,
bursting with yellow brilliance
and with fat, crimson-cheeked confidence
in the new day.

We held a funeral service behind the shed
and I chuckled to myself, thinking of
a small guinea pig springing up one morning
in a furry flurry of brand new life because
you can't hold life back and it moves forward
no matter what.

Bothering Bubby

Bothering Bubby, but today I don't care.
beguiling, sometimes bratty, brave,
beautiful baby brown sugar
in and out of my office
while I am trying to write
but she is only going to be a kid once
and one day when I have gone
away to the four winds
and am only a memory of
a scent, of a time and place
she has almost forgotten,
my little *Neshumele,* my little soul
will think of me and smile, I hope.

The other granddaughter, last night,
was wearing a 50's retro outfit,
"her fashion ethic",
towering over me,
hair flowing, self-assured,
freshly triumphant after
directing a play,
wanting to taste more
of life's adventures,

what will she think about me?
does she think I am a cool Grandma,
or an old relic as I thought of
my own grandparents,
though I loved them?
will I ever know?

I want to tell her how much I love her,
how proud I am, what I see of myself in her,
how I admire what I don't see of myself,
how I accept all that she is and chooses to be,

but she, like many young adults,
doesn't love talking on the phone,
doesn't always answer texts
and only recently let me be her
Facebook friend.

Grandma Speaking Truths

Little brown dumpling has a fleecy cloth book
with textured, silky tags to rub across her
golden cheeks puffed up just the right amount,
warm, almost fresh from the oven.
She lifts soft spongy curls into the breeze
closing eyes with pleasure.

Now I am Medicare Mother, maneuvering
how to be me without dew dozing on perfect skin
and minus smooth-edged roundness that sought
boys and men to sweetly hypnotize.

I speak no Mandarin but if I tell my story
using one word with many tones, will they
always sound the same to men who don't
listen to poems I string together with my
lips and spit out like pomegranate seeds.

I never imagined in my misty dreams with
rain forest thoughts steaming up the mind
that my mother might also have felt this way,
might have needed to hum herself softly
to sleep, alone in the night air till time stopped.

Nine Worlds of Magic

When we sit on footstools, self-constructed,
looking out over all nine worlds of magic,
it is only up to us whether we stand to bravely
catapult over the dark ledge, falling fast, not hard.

We laugh and roll toward tasty promises
already whispering and beckoning like Saturday
morning sleepy sex under the worn white blanket
that a nearly forgotten friend made in another life.

Yet I know many who close heavy lids, weighed down
by habits and choose instead their same old tightly
woven dreams, curling inside them, sad little beetles
in a ball of wet twine downstairs on the cellar shelf.

Over soba noodles we discuss savory options
as though they are spread out in a fan on the table
waiting for us to grab one, wanting us to inhale the
taste of tomorrow and feel dizzy with the tumbling.

I am older now, and have mastered the art of
chopsticks with some Caucasian clumsiness but
still love to tumble, to fly into the colors of the sun
sizzling and sparkling like my birthday rubies.

I dream of beetles ready to wake and make a slow
slimy climb to find me resting on my footstool
My head forgets but nerves have phantom memories
I jump heart-first and fly to land on magic worlds.

I See You, Zalman Grodofsky

I see you, Zalman Grodofsky,
strong young writer at Auschwitz
along with the others, forced labor,
muscled young men, once scholars,
once writers, husbands, fathers,
cold, huddled on the hard bunks
each night inviting the moon to share
in your secret thoughts as you record
them on small paper scraps, sizzling
with the words you want remembered
in yet unborn years, by unborn souls.

Sometimes the moonlight, like life,
is unpredictable, a dull silver sliver
that makes your tired eyes struggle.
Sometimes it sends down milky beams,
peaceful, spreading slowly over paper.
Sometimes eerie, radiant light daggers
attacking dark corners of your universe,
ripping open blackness to reveal
unexpected brilliant stars of hope,
even amidst the unspeakable, which
needs to be written.

You bear witness to more than we read
in history books, you hide bits of Yiddish
in a thermos, in the dirt outside of
the crematoria where you labor by day.
You write instead of sleeping, all that
we can't imagine, and when a new

transport arrives in the inky night,
you pause your moonlight disgorging
of what the world must not forget,
to say kaddish for the arrivals,
whom you've never met.

I awaken now, sick with thoughts
of what is happening in this world.
I write it all in the bright moonlight
of my newest nightmares, fueled by
ugly news that floods our screens,
wondering if the future holds only
a blackened-sky graveyard for the stars,
for our collective hopes and dreams.
I am a woman who says kaddish,
who doesn't care who likes it or not
and I refuse to say it just for Jews.
I don't want to say it for my country.
Can you help me, Zalman Grodofsky?

Old Sorrows, New Poppies

Who doesn't want springtime?
Whose bones are not in a state
of perpetual cold stiffness, yet moving
because we hold an imaginary whip
to make them creak or groan aloud?

Who doesn't need brightness and warmth
to seduce us slowly, till we stretch,
then sigh with almost-forgotten pleasure?
I know I want springtime, but maybe
you're not ready to make the old sorrows
drip with the syrup of new life.

We watch through swirly window designs
painted by the black dog's wet nose.
How soon will we spot the poppies
gone for decades after grief slammed us,
but that now revisit us in spring?

Grief covered our house, dark, slimy algae.
We hostages looked out over barren yard,
scanned it with our eyes, mildly hopeful
in spite of it all, but no poppies chose
to fight a patch out of earth to find the sun.

During sleep, some of you may dream
of red corn poppies, faces tipped up
to sultry afternoon sun, red balloons
of hope, symbols of new life emerging,
of abundance and of scary second chances.

Some people have dreams of black poppies,
opium poppies, symbols of death and doom.
I can tell you, though, that genus papaver,
much like us, returns only when ready
and never sooner, with an array of colors
and ways of showing up in the world.

If too many trees darken poppy potential
they may hide their unrealized brightness
within the cold ground till nature signals
the all-clear, removing any obstacles.
Like us, they are resilient, even when
they don't seem to know it.

If you're not ready for spring,
won't allow your bitter sorrows
to sweeten even one puny drop,
poppies may sprout unseen by you.
You must want to heal, want springtime,
want pain to leave without goodbyes.

You have to want all bare trees left behind
with frozen door locks, slippery ice patches
and with your cold, weary bones.
I know I want springtime, but I'll say again,
maybe you're not ready to make old sorrows
drip with the syrup of new life.

(This poem appeared in an edition of *Red Wolf Journal*.)

Life With Poetry Elves

Poems once poured through cracks
in my crumbling roof of troubles
routinely flooded my soul cellar
yet still kept me afloat when life's
unstable foundation heaved madly
under my cautious footsteps

poems reactivated the sump pump
of my flagging heart
when I watched my loved ones
floating past, barely waving
following beams of soft light
and heavenly nymph music

out of my range of hearing
despite how I longed to hear it
I mustn't think of that now
when I am stuck in dark spaces
pulling gratitude from dusty bags

I know that poems may hide
or tease, those elfin word tricksters
that sit in the tree stumps waiting
to see if I will surrender in defeat
but they never abandon me

Dueling Poets

There are no swords or pistols
as they take designated places
ten yards apart, verses cocked,
one last attempt at reconciliation,
not so much with each other,
but with a cruel world where honor
has too long been besmirched.
In fact, each is already gravely wounded
by this world with its ears tightly sealed
to keep out words falling from dark skies
that once cradled dazzling starts, brightened
hearts, caressed open souls, tickled brains
now filled with endless amusement on screens,
dollar signs and ugly rhetoric and actions
that split open the skull of the human race
till all bleed, forgetting how to feel the magic
of words gifted to us from gods that visit
only in dreams of a very few.

(Two Coaching Poems)
I- Changing Views

When I ask you to reframe,
I know you can't easily change
the colors of your matting
or the wood frame that keeps
the colors safely contained,
stops them from running away,
from not clashing with the couch,
not spilling out into the world.

I know there are so many
who appear to be petals floating
on a pond, drifting with the ducks
not concerned about changing currents
or sooty clouds hanging overhead
where an unknown future hides.

You think they somehow find light,
are transparent, able to easily float
with confidence never known by you.
You think they are spinning ballerinas,
happily fluttering along, never worrying
about unpredictable breezes or
about life's what-ifs.

So I ask gently, with soft cushions
of quiet questions that mount intensity
as you linger less on fears, and begin
a willingness to taste more flavors.

We examine with caution,
instruments warmed at first,
like the cold metal speculum
you've learned to tolerate,
but then we begin to pry apart
the layers where joy has been
concealed, where savages lurk
with hooks that keep you snagged
and hold you back.

***

II- Holding the Space

I will hold the space for you
I will catch it and place it
in a soft web for safekeeping
The web is spun with threads
of answers for which you may
not yet be ready, and with many
questions that could open a door
leading to unimagined meadows

This web is just a doorknob-turn away
around a corner you fear curling into,
a problem you don't yet want to look
in the eye, fearing you will only see
a reflection of your own puzzled face

The explanations you have heard before,
make as much sense as prayers you've sent
up to a deep, dark sky, maybe still unanswered.
The words your mind wants to see in rows
of syllables that line up to march you to clarity,
are not ready to be free, plucked from the web.

You remain in the center, dangling like a tiny fly,
hoping to soon disentangle yourself, to soar out
over the earth to a new adventure

My confidence in you is like a stone wall,
built one rock at a time, strong, dependable,
keeping away what we don't want now,
sheltering spring gardens behind it.
I know you will go where you need to.
I will hold the space, will guard the web
and the tiny flies of doubt in its center.

When the moment seems ripe and juicy,
I will pluck the doubts, hurling them at you,
challenging you to either lose your balance
or to stand up and fly with hope and confidence
So which will it be?

The Ways That I Pray

so very long ago, when living
in slender girl body before life put
sticks and needles into my bedclothes,
I wrote the words, "My poor dull youth
is riding away on horseback while I sleep".

now youth and dullness are thankfully gone.
I seek quiet green spaces or gentle seascapes
that once would have surely bored me.
I practice gratitude that breaks out into
beautiful iridescent bubbles to help me

stay calm and remember my life lessons.
you may know I am not a religious woman.
I find my messages on backs of mourning doves,
my miracles in small dogs, children and wind
tunes that soothe when sleep and I are wrestling.

I pray to the sky, to the water, to the yellow bird
with tiny bones I saw perched on the gazebo,
to smooth stones that sit on the edge of the water.
I pray to whatever being or force has made it all,
and give thanks for having reached this season.

Final Note From Iris

Before you leave, I am sure you have seen that many of the poems in this book focus on grief, loss, aging, but also on hope, survival and determination.

If you are someone who has had a hard time dealing with a significant loss or change, you may have some fears or anxiety about moving in a more positive direction. You may truly *want* to feel better, but something may be holding you back. In your mind, moving ahead may simply be terrifying, but may also represent leaving some things about your past to which you still cling. This may be a loved one who is gone, the "you" who was well before the onset of an illness, the "you" who had certain plans and hopes that seem to have fallen by the wayside for a multitude of reasons.

I understand those fears and the reality that many people experience them. I certainly have at different points in my life. It's a good thing though, to want more peace, comfort, and more creativity and hope in your life. It's a natural thing to want to feel better and do better.

I want to tell you that whatever your reasons for hanging on to what once was, it's time to begin loving yourself and to know that you are worthy of whatever it is you want to feel or do. You really are allowed to feel peace and joy, and even excitement about your life and your future.

In the beginning, when you have had a loss, a disappointment, or what you perceive as a failure, what you most want is just some relief from the sharp, unremitting pain. You just want the torment of the feelings, memories and tears that hurt so badly to stop. For some people, there is anger at themselves, at the world, and even at someone who has died. You really do have to face those things before you are ready to continue on your journey. There is no way around this. The more you push things back, the more likely they are to come screaming up at you at some point. You may or may not be able to deal with this on your own. You may need some help. Getting the right help is a great way of taking care of yourself.

I don't feel that most people need to dwell indefinitely on the past. In fact, I happen to believe that is what keeps many stuck and keeps them from being able to reinvent their lives. A lot of folks may just need some fresh tools to shift their energy and how they think about things.

Whatever has happened to you in the past, there is still a world out there. The sun still comes up, children still laugh and play, music is still being made, art is being created. There are also people out there who need a hug or a smile, or some other kind of help as much as you do. There are cookies to be tasted, words to be written, businesses to be built, and even love in places you may least expect it. You are still alive, and hopefully, have "miles to go before you sleep". When you decide you are ready to notice the world and to change things, you will. You have to make up your mind, for the most part.

I keep telling people to practice. That sounds simplistic, but it's super important. Do even one small thing that is good, pleasurable, and life-affirming today, even if it's for five minutes. Focus on how you feel during those five minutes. What is happening in your body? It will feel very odd at first. You will get better.

I don't know most of you personally, but I do know something about how grief over bad stuff that life deals us can poison our outlooks. It tends to rob us of the present moment and of our futures. This can destroy you, or can make you stronger. It can propel you on to happier and more productive times, if you allow that and if you are willing to do the work.

Please don't waste the rest of your time feeling miserable or angry over things that have happened to you. Take those feelings and figure out how to weave them into a garment of fabulous new colors and textures. If you find you are always angry at others, let it go, because it will eat you alive. Do this in your own time frame, but do it.

If you liked my poetry and thoughts, please tell others and consider posting a review on Amazon.

With love,

Iris J. Arenson-Fuller

Iris J. Arenson-Fuller

Contact

If you would like to contact the author, Iris can be found on the web at:

https://www.visionpoweredcoaching.com

iris@visionpoweredcoaching.com

Glossary

Bubbe also *bubbie, bubby* or *bubba*	*Yiddish* for grandmother
Knish	a large dumpling of dough that is baked or fried and filled with potato, cheese, meat and sometimes fruit
Mandel bread	an oblong cookie, something like biscotti
Manischewitz	a brand of kosher wine
Matzah ball	a type of dumpling often served in chicken soup
Sholem Aleichem	a still beloved *Yiddish* writer who died in 1916, on whose story *Fiddler on the Roof* was based
Zaide also *zaidie, zaidy* or *zaida*	*Yiddish* for grandfather

Iris J. Arenson-Fuller

Made in the USA
Lexington, KY
04 November 2019